Grades K-2

The BRAINY BOOK of Handwriting

Thinking Kids™
An imprint of Carson-Dellosa Publishing LLC
P.O. Box 35665
Greensboro, NC 27425 USA

Thinking Kids™
An imprint of Carson-Dellosa Publishing LLC
P.O. Box 35665
Greensboro, NC 27425 USA

Printed in the USA • All rights reserved.   ISBN 978-1-4838-1329-5
01-113157811

Table of Contents

Let's Warm Up!

Practice by tracing the lines.

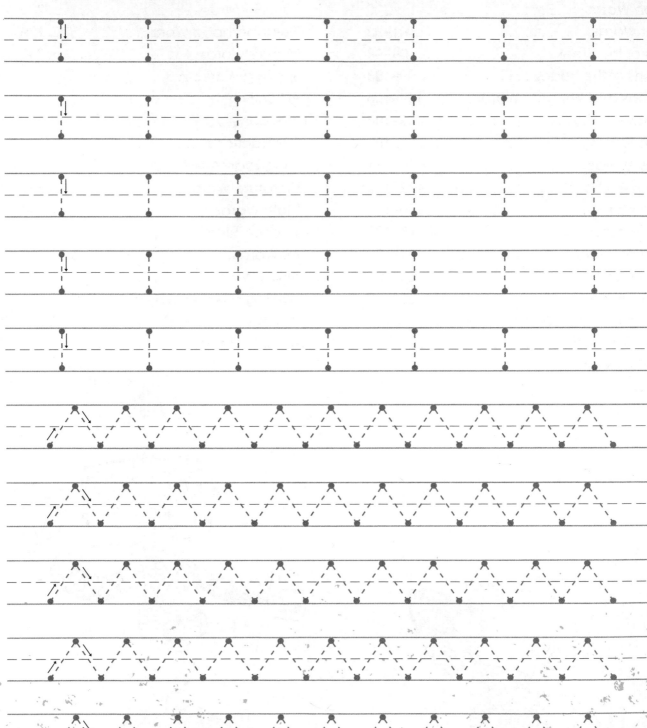

Let's Warm Up!

Practice by tracing the lines.

Let's Warm Up!

Practice by tracing the lines.

Let's Warm Up!

Practice by tracing the lines.

Aa

Practice by tracing the letter. Then, write the letter.

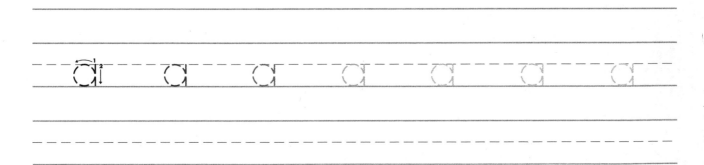

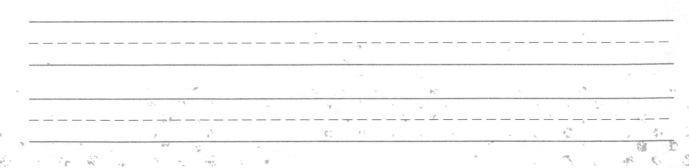

Aa

Practice by tracing the words. Then, write the words.

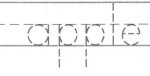

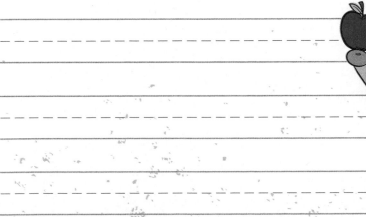

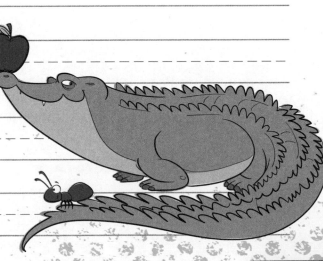

Write the sentence.

Alligators and ants

eat apples.

Bb

Practice by tracing the letter. Then, write the letter.

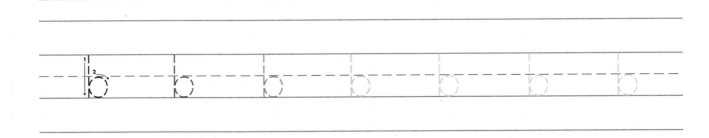

Bb

Practice by tracing the words. Then, write the words.

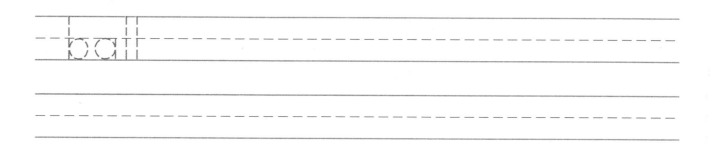

Write the sentence.

Brave Bobby buys a
baseball bat.

Cc

Practice by tracing the letter. Then, write the letter.

C C C C C C C

c c c c c c c

Cc

Practice by tracing the words. Then, write the words.

cats

cookies

cards

Chuck

Cc

Write the sentence.

Cool cats play cards.

Dd

Practice by tracing the letter. Then, write the letter.

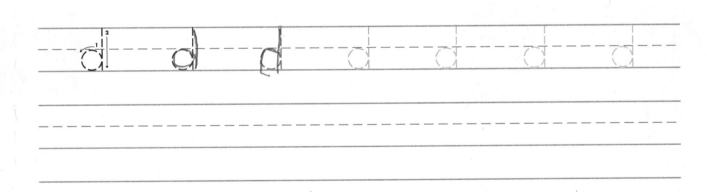

Dd

Practice by tracing the words. Then, write the words.

Dd

Write the sentence.

Danny dances with a
dandy dog.

Ee

Practice by tracing the letter. Then, write the letter.

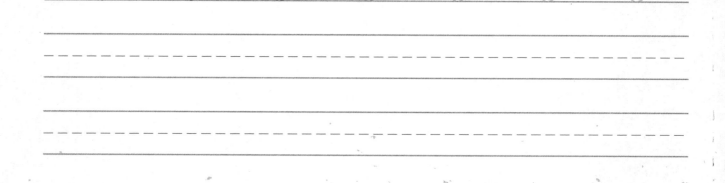

Ff

Practice by tracing the letter. Then, write the letter.

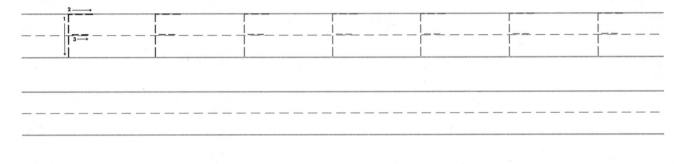

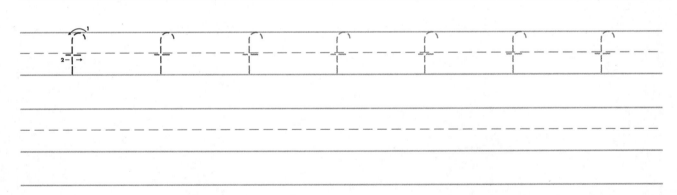

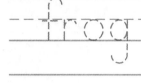

Ff

Practice by tracing the words. Then, write the words.

frog

fish

fox

Florida

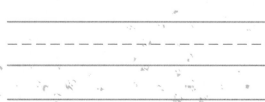

Ff

Write the sentence.

Four foxes and five fish fly
to Florida.

Gg

Practice by tracing the letter. Then, write the letter.

Gg

Practice by tracing the words. Then, write the words.

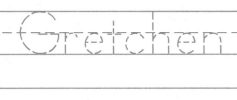

Gg

Write the sentence.

Gretchen wears gray glasses.

Hh

Practice by tracing the letter. Then, write the letter.

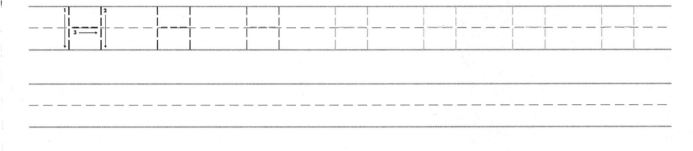

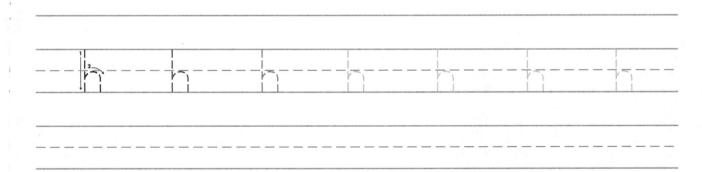

Hh

Practice by tracing the words. Then, write the words.

Hh

Write the sentence.

Hannah hears a hungry hippo.

Ii

Practice by tracing the letter. Then, write the letter.

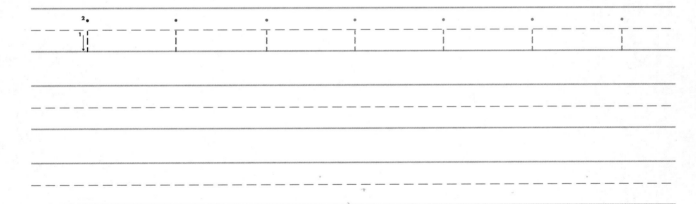

Ii

Practice by tracing the words. Then, write the words.

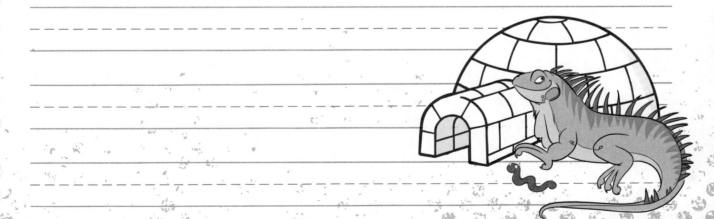

Ii

Write the sentence.

Inchworms itch in Indiana.

Jj

Practice by tracing the letter. Then, write the letter.

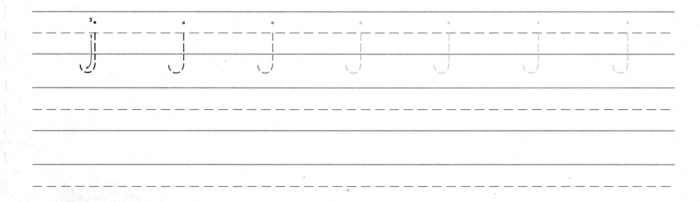

Jj

Practice by tracing the words. Then, write the words.

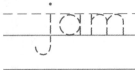

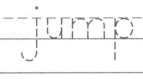

Jj

Write the sentence.

Jumping jaguars tell jolly
jokes.

Kk

Practice by tracing the letter. Then, write the letter.

Kk

Practice by tracing the words. Then, write the words.

kangaroo

kite

key

Kelsey

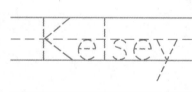

Kk

Write the sentence.

Kind Kelsey keeps

kangaroos.

Practice by tracing the letter. Then, write the letter.

Ll

Practice by tracing the words. Then, write the words.

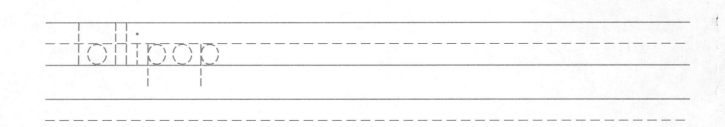

lion

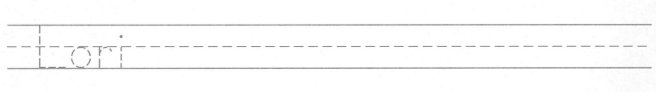

lollipop

lick

Lori

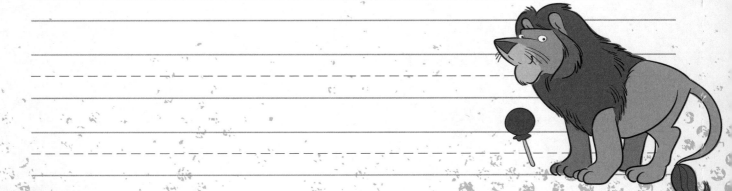

Write the sentence.

Little Lori likes lions and

lollipops.

Mm

Practice by tracing the letter. Then, write the letter.

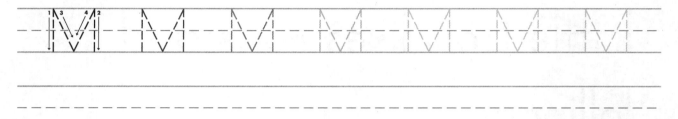

Nn

Practice by tracing the letter. Then, write the letter.

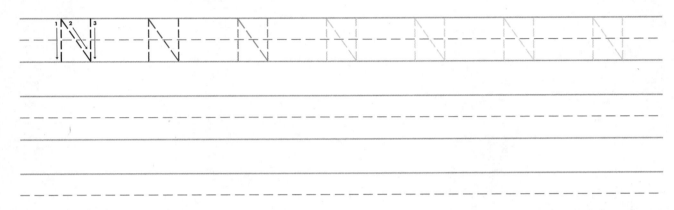

Nn

Practice by tracing the words. Then, write the words.

note

Nn

Write the sentence.

Nine newts have no nest.

Oo

Practice by tracing the letter. Then, write the letter.

Oo

Practice by tracing the words. Then, write the words.

Oo

Write the sentence.

Olivia owns one ostrich and

one octopus.

Pp

Practice by tracing the letter. Then, write the letter.

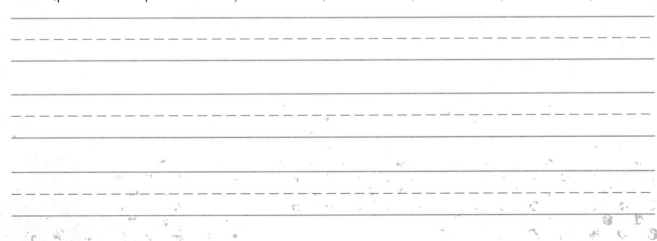

Pp

Practice by tracing the words. Then, write the words.

penguin

pizza

pencil

puppy

Pp

Write the sentence.

The puppy plays in the
pretty pool.

Qq

Practice by tracing the letter. Then, write the letter.

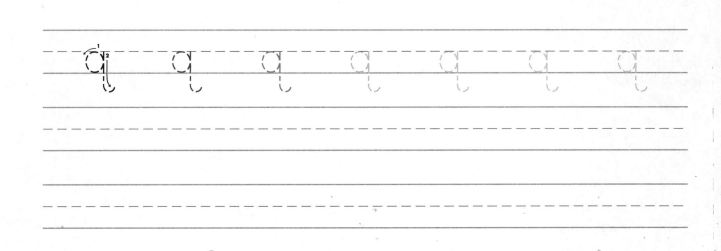

Qq

Practice by tracing the words. Then, write the words.

quail

queen

quarter

quit

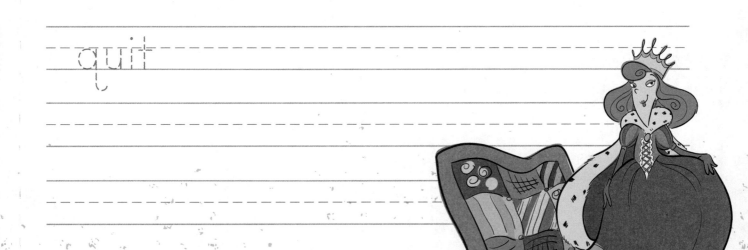

Qq

Write the sentence.

The quiet queen quits quarreling.

Rr

Practice by tracing the letter. Then, write the letter.

Rr

Practice by tracing the words. Then, write the words.

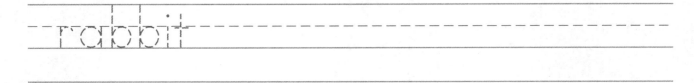

Rr

Write the sentence.

Rowdy rabbits run a road race.

Ss

Practice by tracing the letter. Then, write the letter.

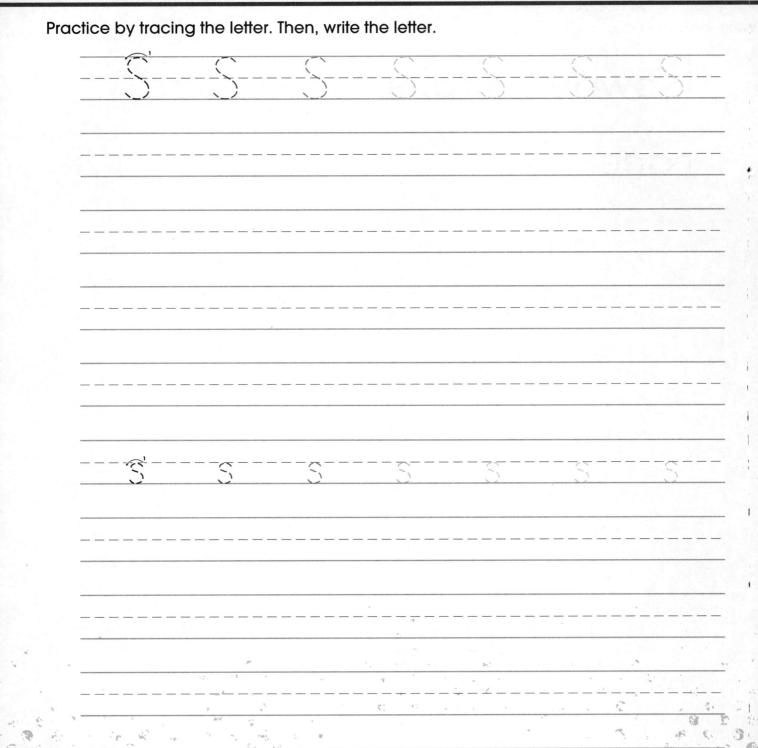

Ss

Practice by tracing the words. Then, write the words.

seal

sun

shell

seven

Ss

Write the sentence.

Seven shells shine in the soft sunshine.

Tt

Practice by tracing the letter. Then, write the letter.

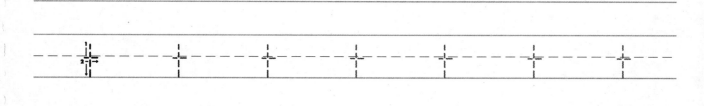

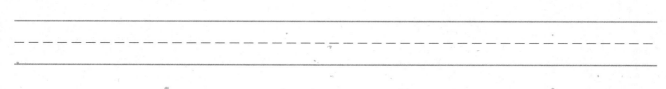

Practice by tracing the words. Then, write the words.

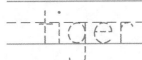

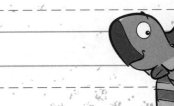

Tt

Write the sentence.

Ten turtles teach tigers.

Uu

Practice by tracing the letter. Then, write the letter.

U   U   U   U   U   U   U

u   u   u   u   u   u   u

Uu

Practice by tracing the words. Then, write the words.

umpire

umbrella

under

unhappy

Uu

Write the sentence.

Unhappy umpires use ugly
umbrellas.

Vv

Practice by tracing the letter. Then, write the letter.

Vv

Practice by tracing the words. Then, write the words.

vulture

violin

vest

van

Vv

Write the sentence.

Vultures in vests play violins.

Ww

Practice by tracing the letter. Then, write the letter.

Brainy Book of Handwriting

Practice by tracing the words. Then, write the words.

Ww

Write the sentence.

A walrus wishes for warm
water.

Xx

Practice by tracing the letter. Then, write the letter.

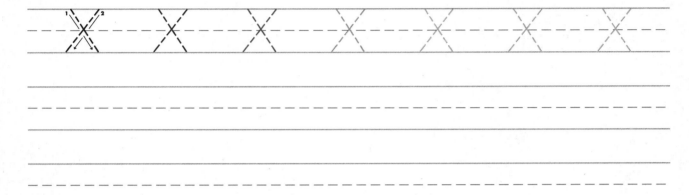

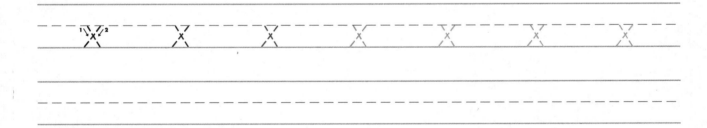

Xx

Practice by tracing the words. Then, write the words.

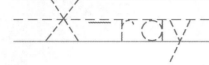

X-ray

Xylophone

Max

Extra

Xx

Write the sentence.

Max got extra xylophones
and saxophones.

Yy

Practice by tracing the letter. Then, write the letter.

Practice by tracing the words. Then, write the words.

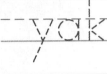

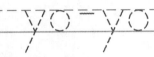

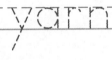

Yy

Write the sentence.

Your yak plays with a
yellow yo-yo.

Zz

Practice by tracing the letter. Then, write the letter.

Zz

Practice by tracing the words. Then, write the words.

zebra

zipper

zoo

zigzag

Zz

Write the sentence.

Zany zebras zigzag through the zoo.

Numbers

Practice by tracing the words and numbers. Then, write the words and numbers.

one 1

two 2

three 3

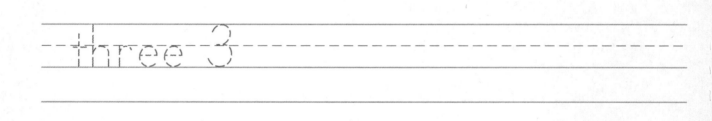

four 4

five 5

Numbers

Practice by tracing the words and numbers. Then, write the words and numbers.

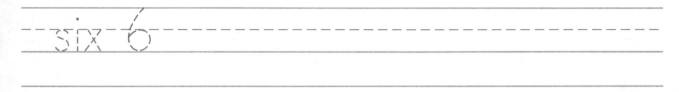

six 6

seven 7

eight 8

nine 9

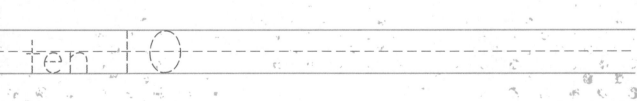

ten 10

Numbers

Practice by tracing the words and numbers. Then, write the words and numbers.

eleven 11

twelve 12

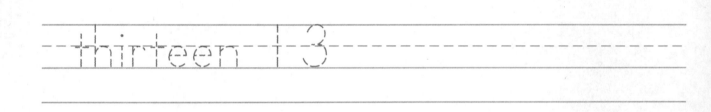

thirteen 13

fourteen 14

fifteen 15

Numbers

Practice by tracing the words and numbers. Then, write the words and numbers.

sixteen 16

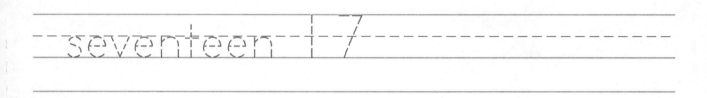

seventeen 17

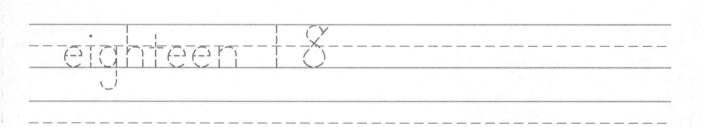

eighteen 18

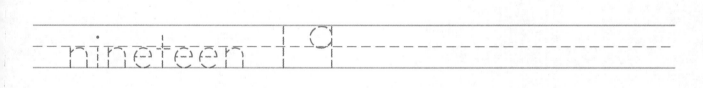

nineteen 19

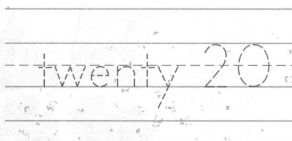

twenty 20

Shape Words

Practice by tracing the words. Then, write the words.

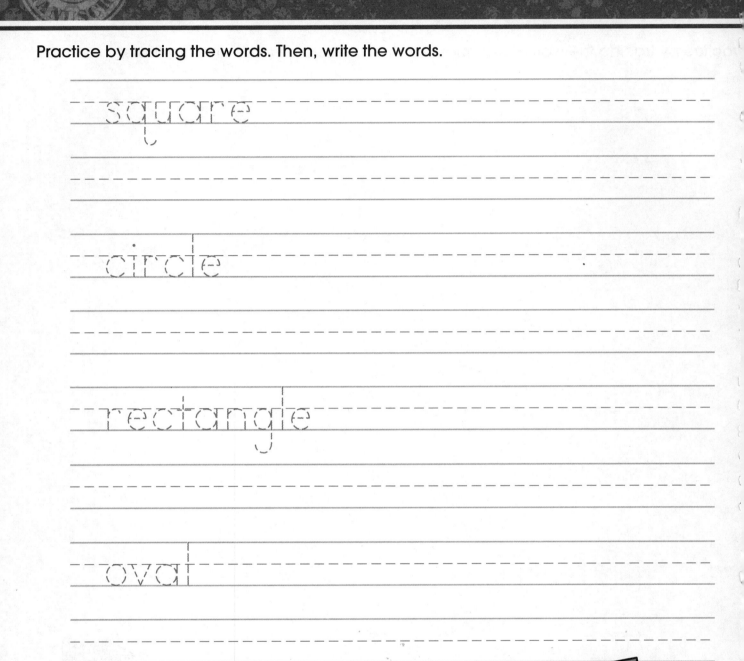

square

circle

rectangle

oval

Brainy Book of Handwriting

Color Words

Practice by tracing the words. Then, write the words.

red

blue

yellow

orange

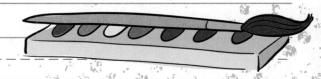

Color Words

Practice by tracing the words. Then, write the words.

 black

 white

purple

 pink

Color Words

Practice by tracing the words. Then, write the words.

brown

gray

green

Complete this sentence:

My favorite color

is _____.

Days of the Week
and Abbreviations

Practice by tracing the words and abbreviations. Then, write the words and abbreviations.

Sunday

Sun.

Monday

Mon.

Days of the Week and Abbreviations

Practice by tracing the words and abbreviations. Then, write the words and abbreviations.

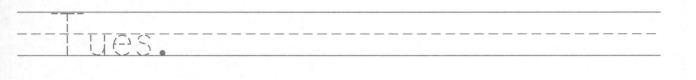

Tuesday

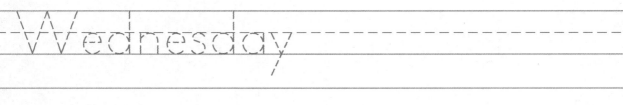

Tues.

Wednesday

Wed.

Days of the Week and Abbreviations

Practice by tracing the words and abbreviations. Then, write the words and abbreviations

Thursday

Thurs.

Friday

Fri.

Days of the Week and Abbreviations

Practice by tracing the words and abbreviations. Then, write the words and abbreviations.

Saturday

Sat.

Today

Name _____

Complete these sentences:

Today is _____.

My birthday is _____.

The 100th day of school is _____.

The Fourth of July is celebrated on _____.

Months of the Year and Abbreviations

Practice by tracing the words and abbreviations. Then, write the words and abbreviations.

January

Jan.

February

Feb.

Months of the Year and Abbreviations

Practice by tracing the words and abbreviations. Then, write the words and abbreviations.

March

Mar.

April

Apr.

Months of the Year and Abbreviations

Practice by tracing the words and abbreviations. Then, write the words and abbreviations.

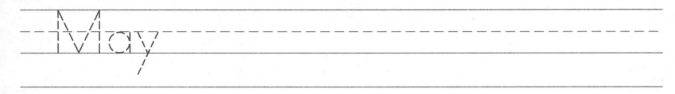

May

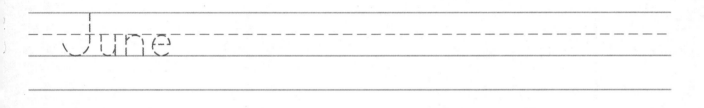

June

July

August

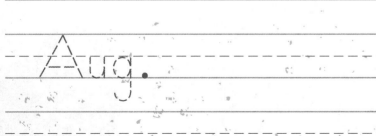

Aug.

Months of the Year and Abbreviations

Practice by tracing the words and abbreviations. Then, write the words and abbreviations

September

Sept.

October

Oct.

Months of the Year and Abbreviations

Practice by tracing the words and abbreviations. Then, write the words and abbreviations.

November

Nov.

December

Dec.

Seasons and Weather Words

Practice by tracing the words. Then, write the words.

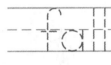

Seasons and Weather Words

Practice by tracing the words. Then, write the words.

snow

rain

sunshine

sleet

Complete this sentence:

Outside, I see _____.

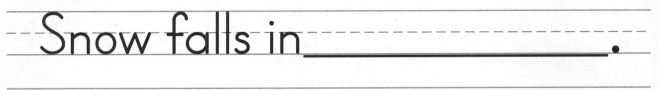

Seasons and Weather Words

Complete these sentences:

Snow falls in_____.

Flowers bloom in_____.

In the_____,

we go swimming.

In the_____, leaves fall.

Holidays

Practice by tracing the words. Then, write the words.

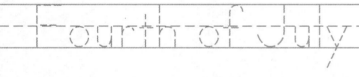

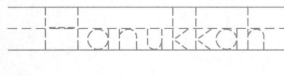

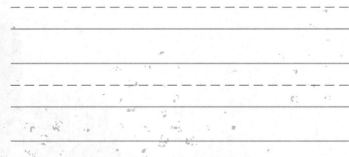

Holidays

Practice by tracing the words. Then, write the words.

Christmas

Thanksgiving

Kwanza

Happy Birthday

Praise Words

Practice by tracing the words. Then, write the words.

awesome

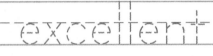

excellent

way to go

great

Safety Words

Practice by tracing the words. Then, write the words.

stop

go

caution

STOP

Safety Words

Complete these sentences:

A_____light means go.

A_____light means stop.

A_____light means

caution.

Family Words

Practice by tracing the words. Then, write the words.

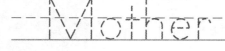

Mother

Father

Mom

Family Words

Practice by tracing the words. Then, write the words.

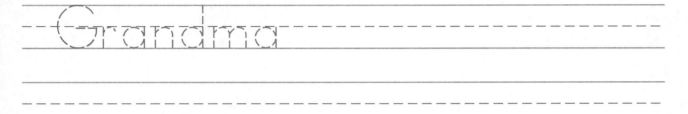

Family Words

Practice by tracing the words. Then, write the words.

aunt

uncle

brother

sister

Family Words

Write the names of the people in your family.

Place Words

Practice by tracing the words. Then, write the words.

country

city

state

town

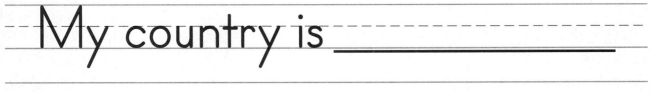

Complete these sentences.

My country is _____

_____ .

My state is _____

_____ .

My town is _____

_____ .

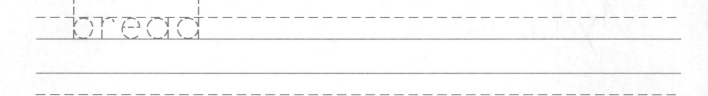

Food Words

Practice by tracing the words. Then, write the words.

bread

meat

vegetable

fruit

Food Words

Practice by tracing the words. Then, write the words.

soup

sandwich

cake

ice cream

Food Words

Complete these sentences.

My favorite foods are

_____

_____ .

If I had a restaurant,

this would be my menu:

_____

_____

_____

_____ .

Direction Words

Practice by tracing the words. Then, write the words.

right

left

up

down

Direction Words

Practice by tracing the words. Then, write the words.

over

under

beside

behind

Sports Words

Practice by tracing the words. Then, write the words.

soccer

football

baseball

golf

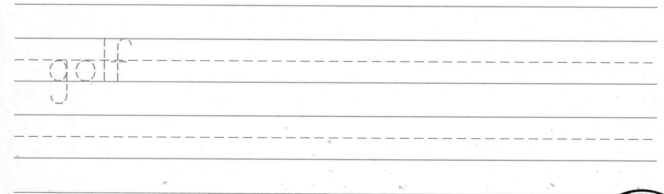

Sports Words

Practice by tracing the words. Then, write the words.

basketball

swimming

volleyball

karate

Sports Words

Practice by tracing the words. Then, write the words.

Sports Words

Practice by tracing the words. Then, write the words.

coach

score

guard

Complete this sentence:

My favorite sport is

Action Words

Practice by tracing the words. Then, write the words.

run

swim

jump

fly

Action Words

Practice by tracing the words. Then, write the words.

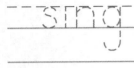

"Writing a Letter" Words

Practice by tracing the words. Then, write the words.

Dear

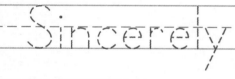

Thank you

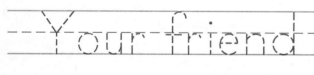

Sincerely

Your friend

Thank-You Note

Practice writing a thank-you note.

Friendly Letter

Practice writing a letter.

Envelope

Practice addressing an envelope.

Aa

Practice by tracing the letter. Then, write the letter.

Aa

Practice by tracing the words. Then, write the words.

an

and

animals

April

Aa

Write the sentence.

Arctic animals act amusingly.

Bb

Practice by tracing the letter. Then, write the letter.

Bb

Practice by tracing the words. Then, write the words.

big

boy

babble

baboon

Bb

Write the sentence.

Big baboons

break balloons.

Cc

Practice by tracing the letter. Then, write the letter.

$\mathcal{C}$ $\mathcal{C}$ $\mathcal{C}$ $\mathcal{C}$ $\mathcal{C}$

$\mathcal{c}$ $\mathcal{c}$ $\mathcal{c}$ $\mathcal{c}$ $\mathcal{c}$

Cc

Practice by tracing the words. Then, write the words.

can

candy

cool

count

Cc

Write the sentence.

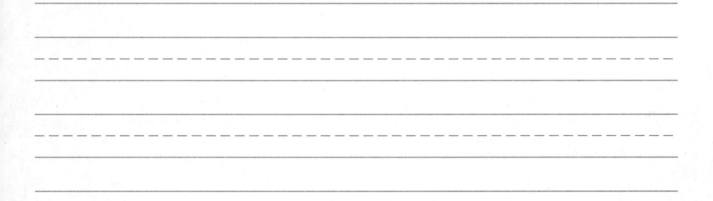

Cool crocodiles count coconuts.

Dd

Practice by tracing the letter. Then, write the letter.

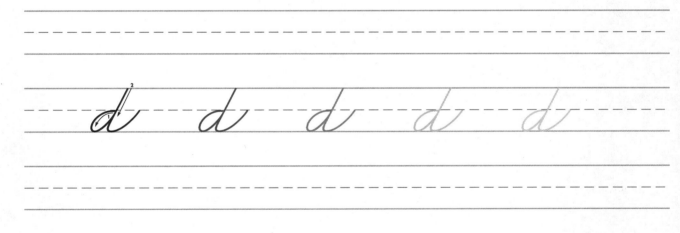

Dd

Practice by tracing the words. Then, write the words.

do

dog

dandelions

donuts

Dd

Write the sentence.

Dogs deliver dandelions and donuts.

Name _____

Ee

Practice by tracing the letter. Then, write the letter.

Brainy Book of Handwriting

Ee

Practice by tracing the words. Then, write the words.

each

eat

eels

eighty

Brainy Book of Handwriting

Ee

Write the sentence.

Electric eels eat excitedly.

Ff

Practice by tracing the letter. Then, write the letter.

Ff

Practice by tracing the words. Then, write the words.

far

fat

fluff

feast

Ff

Write the sentence.

Flamingos fluff fancy feathers.

Gg

Practice by tracing the letter. Then, write the letter.

Gg

Practice by tracing the words. Then, write the words.

gag

gift

good

giggle

Gg

Write the sentence.

Giggling gophers give gag gifts.

Hh

Practice by tracing the letter. Then, write the letter.

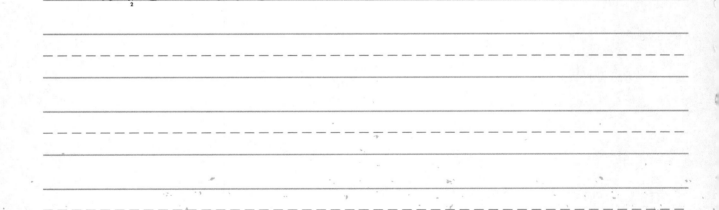

Hh

Practice by tracing the words. Then, write the words.

his

happy

he

hello

Hh

Write the sentence.

Happy hippos hang in their hammocks.

Ii

Practice by tracing the letter. Then, write the letter.

Ii

Practice by tracing the words. Then, write the words.

if

in

idea

itch

Write the sentence.

Insects itch in the infield.

Jj

Practice by tracing the letter. Then, write the letter.

Jj

Practice by tracing the words. Then, write the words.

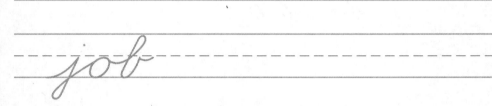

jam

job

jazz

junk

Jj

Write the sentence.

Juggling jaguars jam to jazz.

Kk

Practice by tracing the letter. Then, write the letter.

$\mathcal{K}$ $\mathcal{K}$ $\mathcal{K}$ $\mathcal{K}$ $\mathcal{K}$ $\mathcal{K}$

k k k k k

Kk

Practice by tracing the words. Then, write the words.

kid

key

Kick

keep

Kk

Write the sentence.

Kooky kangaroos

kick in karate.

Ll

Practice by tracing the letter. Then, write the letter.

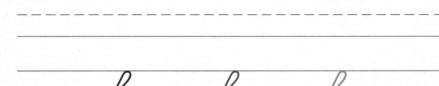

LI

Practice by tracing the words. Then, write the words.

low

land

lamb

little

Ll

Write the sentence.

Little lambs lick lemon lollipops.

Mm

Practice by tracing the letter. Then, write the letter.

Mm

Practice by tracing the words. Then, write the words.

mad

milk

monkeys

merry

Mm

Write the sentence.

Merry monkeys make marmalade.

Nn

Practice by tracing the letter. Then, write the letter.

n n n n n

m m m m m

Brainy Book of Handwriting

Nn

Practice by tracing the words. Then, write the words.

nap

name

near

night

Nn

Write the sentence.

Naughty gnats never nap at night.

Oo

Practice by tracing the letter. Then, write the letter.

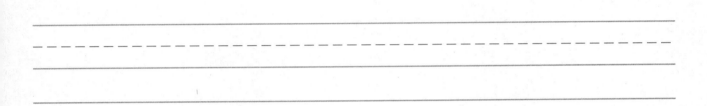

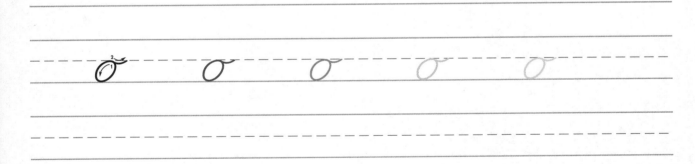

Oo

Practice by tracing the words. Then, write the words.

out

often

once

order

Oo

Write the sentence.

Ostriches often order onion omelettes.

Pp

Practice by tracing the letter. Then, write the letter.

Pp

Practice by tracing the words. Then, write the words.

pan

pet

pick

paper

Write the sentence.

Pandas paint pictures on paper.

Qq

Practice by tracing the letter. Then, write the letter.

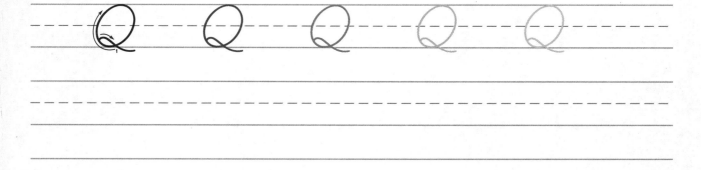

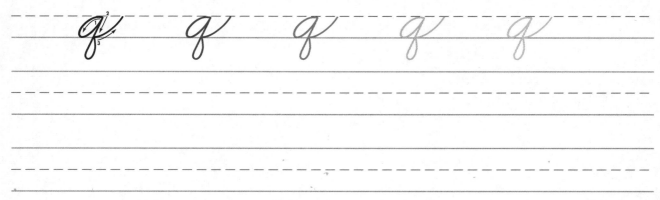

Qq

Practice by tracing the words. Then, write the words.

quit

quick

quart

quiet

Qq

Write the sentence.

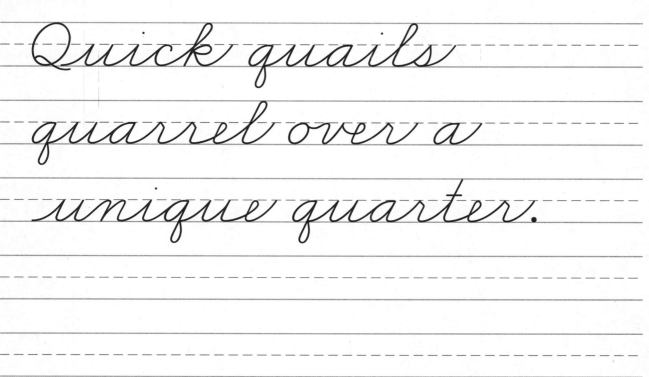

Quick quails quarrel over a unique quarter.

Rr

Practice by tracing the letter. Then, write the letter.

R R R R R

N N N N N

Rr

Practice by tracing the words. Then, write the words.

rat

run

rear

road

Rr

Write the sentence.

Raccoons run races in red cars.

Ss

Practice by tracing the letter. Then, write the letter.

Ss

Practice by tracing the words. Then, write the words.

see

sing

stand

stow

Ss

Write the sentence.

Standing storks

sing with swans.

Tt

Practice by tracing the letter. Then, write the letter.

$\mathcal{T}$ $\mathcal{T}$ $\mathcal{T}$ $\mathcal{T}$ $\mathcal{T}$

t t t t t

Practice by tracing the words. Then, write the words.

the

tip

told

twist

Tt

Write the sentence.

Two tigers tickle each other's toes.

Uu

Practice by tracing the letter. Then, write the letter.

$\mathcal{U}$ $\mathcal{U}$ $\mathcal{U}$ $\mathcal{U}$ $\mathcal{U}$

$\mathcal{u}$ $\mathcal{u}$ $\mathcal{u}$ $\mathcal{u}$ $\mathcal{u}$

Uu

Practice by tracing the words. Then, write the words.

use

under

until

unhappy

Uu

Write the sentence.

Unicorns use umbrellas under thunder.

Vv

Practice by tracing the letter. Then, write the letter.

$\mathcal{V}$ $\mathcal{V}$ $\mathcal{V}$ $\mathcal{V}$ $\mathcal{V}$

$\mathcal{v}$ $\mathcal{v}$ $\mathcal{v}$ $\mathcal{v}$ $\mathcal{v}$

Vv

Practice by tracing the words. Then, write the words.

very

vote

vine

vest

Vv

Write the sentence.

Vultures vacuum in velvet vests.

Ww

Practice by tracing the letter. Then, write the letter.

W W W W W

w w w w w

Ww

Practice by tracing the words. Then, write the words.

wet

west

wall

winter

Ww

Write the sentence.

Wet walruses bowl to win.

Xx

Practice by tracing the letter. Then, write the letter.

Xx

Practice by tracing the words. Then, write the words.

x-ray

box

extra

xylophone

Xx

Write the sentence.

Xandra x-rays boxes with foxes.

Yy

Practice by tracing the letter. Then, write the letter.

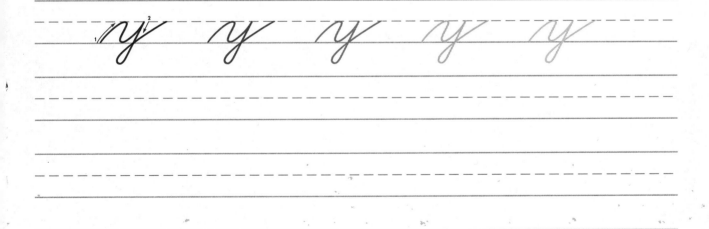

Yy

Practice by tracing the words. Then, write the words.

you

yard

year

yellow

Yy

Write the sentence.

Yaks yell and yodel loudly.

Zz

Practice by tracing the letter. Then, write the letter.

Practice by tracing the words. Then, write the words.

zero

zoom

zone

zipper

Zz

Write the sentence.

Zigzagging zebras zip and zoom.

Numbers

Practice by tracing the words and numbers. Then, write the words and numbers.

one 1

two 2

three 3

four 4

five 5

Numbers

Practice by tracing the words and numbers. Then, write the words and numbers.

six 6

seven 7

eight 8

nine 9

ten 10

Numbers

Practice by tracing the words and numbers. Then, write the words and numbers.

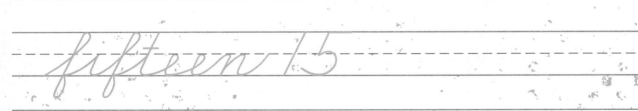

Numbers

Practice by tracing the words and numbers. Then, write the words and numbers.

sixteen 16

seventeen 17

eighteen 18

nineteen 19

twenty 20

Months of the Year and Abbreviations

Practice by tracing the words and abbreviations. Then, write the words and abbreviations.

January

Jan.

February

Feb.

Months of the Year and Abbreviations

Practice by tracing the words and abbreviations. Then, write the words and abbreviations.

March

Mar.

April

Apr.

Brainy Book of Handwriting

Months of the Year and Abbreviations

Practice by tracing the words and abbreviations. Then, write the words and abbreviations.

May

June

July

August

Aug.

Months of the Year and Abbreviations

Practice by tracing the words and abbreviations. Then, write the words and abbreviations.

September

Sept.

October

Oct.

Months of the Year and Abbreviations

Practice by tracing the words and abbreviations. Then, write the words and abbreviations.

November

Nov.

December

Dec.

School Words

Practice by tracing the words. Then, write the words.

gym

playground

classroom

principal's office

School Words

Practice by tracing the words. Then, write the words.

math

music

art

gym

School Words

Practice by tracing the words. Then, write the words.

science

spelling

social studies

writing

School Words

Practice by tracing the words. Then, write the words.

teacher

aide

nurse

principal

School Words

Practice by tracing the words. Then, write the words.

pencil

book

folder

paper

Family Words

Practice by tracing the words. Then, write the words.

Mother

Father

Mom

Family Words

Practice by tracing the words. Then, write the words.

Dad

Grandma

Grandpa

Family Words

Practice by tracing the words. Then, write the words.

aunt

uncle

brother

sister

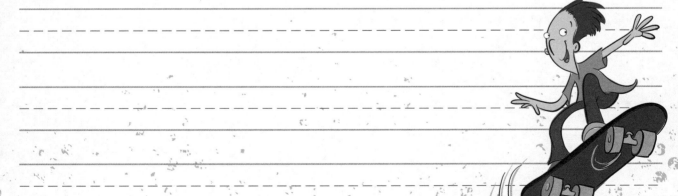

Family Words

Write the names of the people in your family.

Neighborhood Words

Practice by tracing the words. Then, write the words.

street

road

store

theater

Neighborhood Words

Practice by tracing the words. Then, write the words.

apartment

library

office

park

Neighborhood Words

Complete these sentences.

I live in a

My address is

Write a sentence about your neighborhood.

Money Words

Practice by tracing the words. Then, write the words.

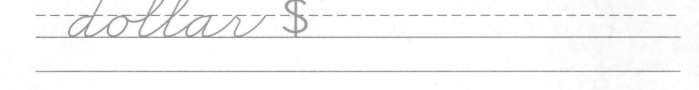

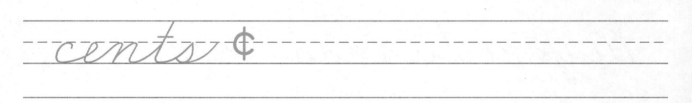

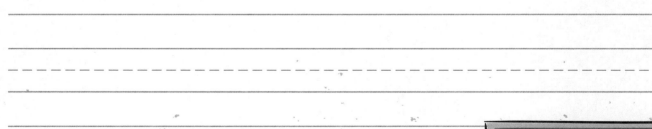

Brainy Book of Handwriting

Money Words

Practice by tracing the words. Then, write the words.

nickel 5¢

dime 10¢

quarter 25¢

Money Words

Write the name of the coin underneath each picture.

_____

- - - - - - - - - - - - - - - - - - -

_____

_____

- - - - - - - - - - - - - - - - - - -

_____

_____

- - - - - - - - - - - - - - - - - - -

_____

_____

- - - - - - - - - - - - - - - - - - -

_____

_____

- - - - - - - - - - - - - - - - - - -

_____

_____

- - - - - - - - - - - - - - - - - - -

_____

_____

- - - - - - - - - - - - - - - - - - -

_____

_____

- - - - - - - - - - - - - - - - - - -

_____

_____

- - - - - - - - - - - - - - - - - - -

_____

_____

- - - - - - - - - - - - - - - - - - -

_____

Spelling Words

Practice by tracing the words. Then, write the words.

dictionary

definition

alphabetical order

Name _____

Adjectives

Practice by tracing the words. Then, write the words.

big

long

tall

good

236

Brainy Book of Handwriting

Pronouns

Practice by tracing the words. Then, write the words.

I

me

you

her

we

Pronouns

Practice by tracing the words. Then, write the words.

he

she

they

them

Brainy Book of Handwriting

Contractions

Practice by tracing the words. Then, write the words.

I'll

she'll

we'll

you'll

Language Arts Words

Practice by tracing the words. Then, write the words.

sentence

paragraph

poem

story

Language Arts Words

Complete these sentences.

At the end of a

_____, *you*

put a period.

A _____

has a main idea.

A _____ *does not*

have to rhyme.

A _____ *has a*

beginning, middle,

and end.

Literature Words

Practice by tracing the words. Then, write the words.

fiction

nonfiction

biography

autobiography

Brainy Book of Handwriting

Literature Words

Complete these sentences.

A _____ book

tells about things

that really

happened.

A _____ book

tells a story

that is not real.

A _____

tells the story of

someone's life.

Math Words

Practice by tracing the words. Then, write the words.

add

subtract

multiply

divide

Math Words

Practice by tracing the words. Then, write the words.

sum

product

regrouping

Complete this sentence:

When you add,
the answer is
called a _____.

Math Words

Practice by tracing the words. Then, write the words.

Math Words

Use words from the previous page to complete these sentences.

There is _____

glass of milk left.

The pizza is

_____

gone.

There is only

_____ of the

pizza left.

Math Words

Practice by tracing the words. Then, write the words.

yard

inch

foot

mile

meter

Math Words

Complete these senetences.

There are three feet in a _____.

There are twelve _____ in a _____.

There are thirty-six inches in a _____.

There are 1,760 yards in a _____.

Science Words

Practice by tracing the words. Then, write the words.

habitat

experiment

food chain

water cycle

Art Words

Practice by tracing the words. Then, write the words.

paint

draw

sketch

sculpture

Music Words

Practice by tracing the words. Then, write the words.

sing

piano

note

strings

Music Words

Practice by tracing the words. Then, write the words.

band

violin

drums

trumpet

"Writing a Letter" Words

Practice by tracing the words. Then, write the words.

Dear

Thank you

Sincerely

Your friend

Thank-You Note

Practice writing a thank-you note.

Friendly Letter

Practice writing a letter to a friend.